Breakfast for the Birds

poems by

Jude Marr

Finishing Line Press
Georgetown, Kentucky

Breakfast for the Birds

For Tom

Copyright © 2017 by Jude Marr
ISBN 978-1-63534-206-2 First Edition
All rights reserved under International and Pan-American Copyright Conventions.
No part of this book may be reproduced in any manner whatsoever without written permission from the publisher, except in the case of brief quotations embodied in critical articles and reviews.

ACKNOWLEDGMENTS

The following poems, sometimes in different form, were previously published:

"Graveyard Shift" in *Concīs Magazine*
"It's a Guy Thing" in *Cactus Heart*
"Cross-Town" in *Mojave River Review*
"After You Come at the Appointed Time" in *Rufous City Review*
"Breakfast for the Birds" in *Kenning Journal*
"Inquire Within: A Reader's Guide" in *Cherry Tree*
"Absent Friends" in *Southern Pacific Review*
"Casablanca, 1942," "Groucho Alone," "Three Days in Fall," and "Sigmund in London" in *The Tower Journal*
"As the Soldier Reloads" in *Sugared Water*
"Wild Nights" and "When I Wake Up with Dread" in *Typoetic.us*
"#1 Haircut," and "You Ask Me, Where Did I Come From?" in *Black Heart Magazine*
"Elegy For a Mother Who May Be Dead" and "Geography and Interior" in *Lost Coast Review*
"Climbing Out of Downtown" in *Words Dance*
"Night Train" in *Lyre Lyre*
"Immortality" in *The Cortland Review*
"Landscape, Interrupted" in *Bird's Thumb*
"Auto-Biography of Miss Jane Doe" in *r.kv.ry Quarterly Literary Journal*
"I Am" and "Fish in the Milk" in *In/Word*
"Flight—" in *Really System*

Publisher: Leah Maines

Editor: Christen Kincaid

Cover Art: Martha Andrews

Author Photo: Anne Hill DeCarteret

Cover Design: Elizabeth Maines McCleavy

Printed in the USA on acid-free paper.
Order online: www.finishinglinepress.com
　　　　　also available on amazon.com

Author inquiries and mail orders:
Finishing Line Press
P. O. Box 1626
Georgetown, Kentucky 40324
U. S. A.

Table of Contents

Graveyard Shift	1
It's a Guy Thing	2
Cross-Town	3
After You Come at the Appointed Time	4
Interiority	5
Breakfast for the Birds	6
You Ask Me, Where Did I Come From?	7
Inquire Within: A Reader's Guide	8
Fish in the Milk	9
Absent Friends	10
La Journée	11
Sunset at the Equator	13
Casablanca, 1942	14
As the Soldier Reloads	15
Sigmund in London	16
Groucho Alone	17
Wild Nights	18
#1 Haircut	19
A Wet Day in the Village	20
Elegy for a Mother Who May Be Dead	21
Geography and Interior	22
Climbing Out of Downtown	23
Night Train	24
Immortality	25
Landscape, Interrupted	26
Auto-Biography of Miss Jane Doe	27
Three Days in Fall	29
I Am	30
Flight—	31
When I Wake Up with Dread	32

Graveyard Shift

sleep fells me with a sucker punch
to the head: I fall for it
forfeit a waste of days in favor
of elephants dreamed—

a pachyderm herd
gray hides a tracery
trunks a tidal wave of gray—

awake: rays nail me to a pillow: yellow
spreads across my sham. Another damn—

egrets perch, smears of white
on swaying gray—elephants as fodder
for a bird of parasites: tusks
as weaponry—

my lids won't close: I am nose to nose
with elephant: a tusk nudges
my skull: *I am not*
my scars, I say—

elephant's eye-glint
impales. Her ear's a ragged flap. *Scars*
are us, she answers back.

It's a Guy Thing

Women always cry, my dad said. But I never
once saw his mother weep,
not even in anger, not even
when her blue-eyed boy spat on me
(don't know why, guess
I reminded him)—
                                not even
when my knuckleheaded brother
traded his class ring for a knife,
chose another life because a swagger
in half-mast pants
called him a name I still can't get
my mouth around—
                                     (blunt)
instruments leave bruises. Tissue tears.
Bone withers in the aftermath.
I wipe my face on your sleeve
before you go.

Cross-Town

two buses and a subway crush to get
to Red Hook, and—

Amanda, friend

      who could make
      a torn tee shirt breathe: friend whose sleeve
      smelled of consolation, back when
      batter hugged the bowl's curve
      and every afternoon ran, arms wide, toward cake—

Mandy, sitting in state with fifty candles, does not
unwrap the gift I have flown six hundred miles
to deliver—

my hand, curled
around her wrist.

After You Come at the Appointed Time

rain smacks
against a pitched roof
rhythmic
as finger-drum:

when you bite my bottom lip: when your hip
grinds me
between bed and bored: I try
to lie straight—imagine space
between each vertebra:
from cervical to sacral curve
a screw unscrewed—

I try, but still
my upper spine contracts
into a jointed shrug: when I hug
my knees, close
against my hollowed chest, you rest—

stewed sheet-roil sets
around our lees—

and then: when
your glittery fingers curl
around my thigh, I am
owned again

then free:

After. You leave. Then, me.

Interiority

I have missed this.

Sitting with a blank page.

Staring at   spaces
         feinting   at a lazy
fly—

I have missed making waves
in cooled coffee—spoon-jiggle as displacement—
spilt milk as metaphor—

last week, I lost traction in quotidian sludge,
my train derailed—every semi-scheme
jackknifed—
Christ.

I should go to the store,
before it closes. I should make a list.

A quiet mind.
A sharpened pencil.
Wits.

Breakfast for the Birds

in intimate circles I am known not
by my heart's circumference
but rather by the jut of my chin—

mornings I push my fist into a knotted pillow
and move my left hip into a different discomfort—

you said: don't sleep with your heart
pressed against an inanimate object

and I stood by an open window and sawed
my last bagel into breakfast for the birds—

I know bone-wired and helpless
from past lives
and still obsession leads me back
to rope and road
to backwoods shack and
solitary
idleness of dappled birch
and docile weeds—

my heart's a muscle without memory
a sparrow-sized anomaly
beating from thought to thought—

on Christopher Street
Con-Ed is digging a hole.

I think about how your ass looks in jeans.

I am a thundering pulse.

You Ask Me, Where Did I Come From?

And I say, I was born
in a trunk. In a punched tin steamer trunk
stowed in the hold of an ocean-going
womb. And I say, my trunk wore
a coat of cream paint overlaid with decals
from every port I'll ever call home.
And my trunk had a leather hasp
and a padlock of chrome.
And I don't say, but you know
that my trunk's my snail shell now, although
sharp-cornered. And my trunk's a sprung
trap for photographs and handkerchiefs
folded in tissue and naphthalene.
And my trunk's always filled
with items not wanted on voyage.
And some day you won't be with me
when my trunk is upended
on a quay in another country. You ask me, how
did I arrive? And I say, (and when I
leave, likewise) as cargo.

Inquire Within: A Reader's Guide

Stacks of modernists, haphazard, on a window ledge. The Macbeths
wedged by Webster, Roget, Kael—anthologies, collected plays,
unopened mail—
                                                  Daisy and Jay, alone.

Rehearsal copies of *Godot*—and *Finnegan*, buried
under un-read Proust. Doctor Seuss. Then Alice, aged and acid
hard by Nabokov—

A separate shelf for histories of the Holocaust.

Titanic tales, treacherous whales, *Infinite Jest*.
Rights of Man, The Second Sex—
and an academy of poets: rows of rough beasts
slouching, spines cracked, across twelve centuries of rage—

Also a Bible, calf-skinned, gilt-edged, kept for language' sake,
not because someone—long dead—wrote on the flyleaf:
                                                  Go with God.

Fish in the Milk

Circumstances
have upended me
into opacity.

Not swimming
but clowning.

Seriously, I may be
drowning.

But if, on a scale
of one up to infinity
I'm a three—

still as I dive
I see the pitcher
and the bowl.

Absent Friends

easy for me to leave
with lines unsaid—

leave a loaned key
brass-bold
on a nightstand
with a note that explains
nothing

leave on a whim
in a cab
after breakfast or dinner
or in between
arguments

leave behind a book
already read or a sweater
with holes too big
to fit in a single bag—

and when I overnight
airside, or in an alien
motel, I may recall
Don Quixote
or hear again a speech
of Vladimir's and wonder
if you're cold—

or I may fall
asleep as easily
as I grow old.

La Journée

Café au lait, sugarless,
taken at a sidewalk table
on the Rue des Dames. Tout
le monde passes by as I dunk
my last ginger cookie, smooth
my flattop, part pinked lips—

Midday, Gare de Lyon. Body-clots
slug into a southbound train.
A snip in a spangled halter-top
tugs on her Daddy's sleeve. She
points. *C'est un gamin?* she says.
I grip my garment bag—

Dinner in Nice (*escargots à l'ail*
followed by bouillabaisse).
A close-shaved purse-puppy,
dwarfed by bows, shivers in Chanel
at the bar. I read de Beauvoir
while boys pose as sluts—

Antibes. A nightcap. Absinthe,
dash of Perrier. Salt-laden
slap of waves, stars
scattershot across a fustian sky.
I shell pistachios. Under
my skin, I'm in disguise—

Midnight. Bent elbows
crease my silk tuxedo. Not
some chic little number
every Ms is meant to covet. My
pants hang suspendered. Gendered.
Zipper-flied. I stride—

La Grande Corniche. A mistral
blow exposes crisp Egyptian cotton
pierced by onyx-inlaid antique
studs. My heart's hard
against a paisley-patterned vest.
Ahead, an open road.

Sunset at the Equator

A livid disc
drops
onto Singapore—
crimson kamikaze.
Night
thickens to pitch.

At Changi, in a marbled
transit lounge, a trio plays
Gershwin hits. CNN
mouths terror
and apocalypse
to traveler ants. Ice kisses
a martini glass.

Love, it seems, is here to stay.

Across runways—another
Changi. A prison, unseen, under
curfew. A continuity
of crowded cells
stacked
over Empire's bones.

Ours, theirs—

but no one talks
about that war
anymore.

Enola Gay, Enola Gay.

Long ago (and far away).

Casablanca, 1942

At *Rick's Café,* America is
Bogey, acting tough: his frontier
lonesomeness wisecracks
toward a beautiful friendship.

In his dressing room, Bogart takes
a call. Not from Bacall. Not yet.
But Ilsa and Rick
will always have Burbank.

Heydrich is dead. The *Blue Parrot's*
a backlot mirage. Only the bird
is real. While Renault memorizes,
Victor Laszlo eats lunch alone.

London is in flames.
Peter Lorre holds a cigarette
between yellowed fingers. Smoke
skeins linger around his head.

Paris. A city caged.
The *Marseillaise* turns extras into refugees
from Central Casting.
Beyond the soundstage, a desert.

A cardboard plane awaits Ilsa's
regret. Our hero wears a trench-coat
over his tuxedo. He tilts
his fedora toward a hill of beans.

Sam can't play piano. He never learned.
But you must remember this.
In Warsaw, in the ghetto,
they are rounding up the usual suspects.

As the Soldier Reloads

winter, bone-cold, creeps in
between
the stitches of my coat

at my throat, a hand—my
hand but—barely
a pulse—blood, stiff
between bitter fingers—

I am not
abandoned: only overcast
by branches

how I stand I can't tell: snow
my exoskeleton: flurries

spit in my face
I am blinded by flakes—

(a star explodes)

all I know: a punctured
sky: a pit below.

Sigmund in London

His Hampstead study is Vienna rebuilt
in homage to guilt by free association.
Freud is eighty-two and ill. Facing east
he can still hear his books burning, or
see his sisters, who have no exit visas.

Patients sometimes call. His couch
leaks confidences. When he wakes
from a painless dream, Freud feels
his daughter's love like scrim
draped over a raddled, raw-boned face.

His cancer cannot be excised from
a mouth made tumorous by smoke.
Sometimes, beyond pleasure, a cigar is
just destruction in a gaudy wrapper.
His doctor lies, but Sigmund knows.

Agony blasts ego into id, but Dr. Freud
is an heroic thinker. His ruined jaw
makes an oh. His physician has promised
morphine, but the analyst's child may say
no. What does a woman want, after all?

Groucho Alone

No kohl-black mustache
slicked across a backstage pallor
bleached by klieg. Only
autumn's grizzle, sun-blushed,
and a balding head
rested against infinities
of rusty brick—

A willow tree, a mockingbird, a gardener's *schtick*—
paradise, you could say.

Wild Nights

I stand in the bathtub and listen to rain
pounding my yard

lightning branches blossom
thunder drums

I am a trumpet vine
my mouth upturned to the showerhead

my petals shed

I am   unmoored.

#1 Haircut

The way gray grows
like mold
over an unremembered loaf
reminds me I will never be
nineteen again.

The buzz of clippers
clearing my head
        (I am a scythed figure
        in a cloud of bees)
defines me.

Until, in glass, I see
my dad, reanimated.

A Wet Day in the Village

Coffee-shop rattle and hiss, storm-threats
set to Wynton Marsalis—
espresso steam meets overcoat.

You shake your umbrella.

I order. I pay. You claim the easiest chair.
Somebody up there loves us, you say,
blowing froth off your macchiato.

I sip while you gossip.

Your hip implant's settling in
but you still can't kneel. Jim's depressed.
And Lou—from across the street—labeled
your plumber *that African* again—

I retie one shoestring (double-knotted). I
chew on a chocolate biscotti.

The new kitchen's a doozy. You had
to remodel, of course, post-inundation,
which shows how good things
sometimes come to those who suffer.
And now you have a tankless heater—

A cinnamon-skinned boy has come
to rest against your elbow. You lean
toward me. Coffee breath. A fleck
of spittle. *Save me from the African,*
you whisper.

Coffee shop rattle and hiss.
Wynton Marsalis at Lincoln Center.

Elegy for a Mother Who May Be Dead

I left you at the corner of here
and there
                      I, leaning into the wind

you, silent
over downtown clank and rattle
over cross streets
over hum—

                      the crazy woman
                      outside the Korean grocery
                      gave me a paper flower

                      every day for a year

                      petals fell like ash
                      after conflagration

and here
                      I kick through drifts
                      of discarded antipathies

—are you still there?

Geography and Interior

A flat planet pinned to a classroom wall. Nations named and claimed.
And me, aching to be where there be dragons.

Earth's a ball caught in a net. Lines intersect. I long for latitude.
For a bellied sail and a spyglass—

Pain's a constant now. Dragons' teeth tear at my concentration.
Loss, like a bird, sings inside my chest.

I am confined. My mind reduced to wordplay.
If I sail away, if I let pain take me to another place—

When I close my eyes against the glare I see a universe of floating worlds
black dots adrift in crimson space—

I cannot rest. I cannot trace my route from here
to where the anchor's weighed.

Climbing Out of Downtown

Scrape sky off of your shoe.
Pull weeds out of your hair. Wear
gray fatigues.
City streets bleed dust. You will
disappear—

Hear greed spill into cracks. Don't
look back. Don't
relax. Wind wire around your heart. Be
smart. Never
unplug used from user. Choose
a room without windows—

Wind blows. Garbage
huddles under
bridges.

River stink, brackish
between broken piers. Birdlime smeared
along your cheek. A parapet—

Hold winter in a close embrace.
Under a star-scoured canopy of ironwork
face north and taste
the bittersweet of Charon's kiss.
Remember this.

The rest, forget.

Night Train

Leave heat-sapped city people eating cart food, grease
hiss-dripping onto skillet-slabs. Leave
angry cabs stranded in stagnant traffic. Pick up
your bags and go
                        to Penn Station. Descend
to where, revivified by cryogenic air, hardiest travelers
ensnare redcaps while untended lines take root beneath
a leafless Garden. Arm yourself with a tall chai, a Panini
and a magazine, then tack
                            toward the great departures
board where schedules harden, where unheeded clicks
determine onward journeys. Negotiate a safe route
around haggard glances, rictus-lips and last-grasp hands
to reach that damned escalator. Leave
                                all bright-light
busyness behind. Leave aspiration.
                        Descend again
to where your conductor awaits.

Immortality

I died.
I am ash scattered,
half-heartedly, across
a parking lot
by my sister's boy, who looks
like her, not me. He is not
my legacy. Winds
have sown my least substantial parts
at the edge of a tarmac
blanket—my dust will
nourish weeds.

I did not die.
Machines
breathed for me, while tender
cuts separated flesh
from flesh.
Quick hands proved
my vital organs. Science
dispatched me,
dry-iced,
to answer prayers—

my heart still beats.

Landscape, Interrupted

a shirttail-sail swells
desert-bright and blooming
around a dead boy's desiccated ribs

boy's story: glory, sacrificed

no tears

know this:
pity's barbs won't corral
suffering, or shred
old scripts—

Auto-Biography of Miss Jane Doe

Archaeology rescued J. Doe's remains
from a re-zoned potter's field, before the backhoes
flattened clods into the basis for a co-ed dorm—

*dirt-rain muck-churned mud-red on midwife's boot sheet-reek and
mama dyed at my first wake*

Pathology measured Doe at fifty-seven inches
and an estimated twenty years. Her diseased joints,
her skull's deformity, screamed tertiary syphilis—

*my Rory my beau lost at sea Rory raw and bonny rest his soul Rory
made May maid no more*

History judged, from the situation of the grave
and the condition of the bones, that Jane Doe must have lived
a whore, before post-Reconstruction's Gilded Age—

*pa traded me for meat plucked fowl blood sausage mutton rare
sweet not spoiled not like pa's wee May*

Women's Studies gave Ms Doe more shape: urban slum child,
further pauperized by gender; tender cherry-
flesh broken/sold/assaulted by misogyny; face made hideous by
pox—

*nor bairn's nor women's sickness dosed with mercury I shrink from
sticks and staines from stink from me*

Art played with Jane. Art digitized her skull, repaired
the syphilitic parts, layered virtual clay. Maybe J's
reconstructed face, her blunt unwholesomeness, failed
to inspire; still, Art clicked SAVE—

*tenement bed-wretched breath blood coughed consumption they say
can't wake May*

Meanwhile, Buildings and Grounds scheduled another hole (fifty-seven inches—four-foot-nine) and re-buried Unidentified Human Remains, Female #63.

dirt-rain muck-churned mud-red on digger's boot

Moral Philosophy may plant a cherry tree at her feet—

who says amen wakes me

Three Days in Fall

Should I bring out my dead on this day
devoted to defiance? Another skeleton
or two—who'd notice? While pumpkin
skulls grin from porch rails and kids in
bone bodysuits go door-to-door, who'd
know my ghosts for what they are, what
they always were—shades unmourned?

Tomorrow creeps on. Maybe saints stand,
ready to be praised. Maybe they pass pagan
wraiths in midnight's hallway, feel superior,
or maybe they simply give way. My face
is still painted, ghastly pale. Maybe my
careless yesterdays can masquerade as
failure. Maybe I'll be wracked, or pinioned—

Darkness again, and I see I have no aptitude
for sanctity. No angels wait; no costume-party
demons, eager to ease pitchforks into so-
solid flesh. Star-points flash, signaling
deaths too distant, too seemingly merciful
to quiet consciousness. Mortal remains
mortal. No souls will light my dusty road.

I Am

not Descartes, warming my feet at the stove,
wine cup in hand, sopped bread ready to entice,
spiced to satisfy; I don't have to agonize; I am
willing to accept my existence as a working
hypothesis.
                I am relatively sure (sure as can
be squared with a care-less universe) that there's
right and wrong, one mensch to another; when
I am bleeding, my sister, my brother, be
my Band-Aid.
              I am not perfect, Plato knows, but
I am trying to be sentient; seeing believes, but my
reality is in my fingertips; my love, when I touch
your face, your fire lights me. Your breath
intoxicates.
             I am a glow in deep
space, an existential spark defined by darkness;
Nietzsche is dead; my friend, cup your hand around
my frail flame; watch over me until I am nothing
but carbon again.

Flight—

an act of will, defiance
of earth's apron strings—

a contrail, swipe of hope
across abraded sky—

a promise of release
from grave imaginings—

a trace of immortality, windhover
still, between fear's fall and rise—

a pact with gods: the physics
of deflected prayer—

or jet-fueled arrows aimed, sensate—
and bodies, falling, everywhere.

When I Wake Up with Dread

six a.m.

day clawing at the drapes

and refrigerator grind is an empty mind
dry-heaving acid aftertaste

sometimes I forget to breathe—

you are not
a tangled comforter
and you are not

soft blues
still playing

and you are not a phone alarm

no, dread

you are a butterfly regressed to larval creep
inside my sleep-stunned belly

but here's the thing

I'm awake now.
I need you to be winged.

Jude Marr was born in Dundee, Scotland, in 1958. After a career in librarianship, followed by twelve years of writing and drifting, she arrived in the United States in 2011 to study for an MFA at Georgia College in Milledgeville. In 2015, she became a PhD student at the University of Louisiana at Lafayette where she also teaches, and works in the Writing Center. Her poetry has appeared in *The Cortland Review, Black Heart Magazine,* and *Cherry Tree* among others, and in 2014, she received an honorable mention for her submission to the Frankye Davis Mayes Prize sponsored by the Academy of American Poets. Jude was selected for the first ever *One Story* Summer Workshop in 2010, proving that she does sometimes write fiction. She has also participated in the Bread Loaf Translators' Conference, Martha's Vineyard Writers' Residency, and the Palm Beach Poetry Festival. She is currently poetry editor for the online journal *r.kv.ry*.

www.ingramcontent.com/pod-product-compliance
Lightning Source LLC
LaVergne TN
LVHW050046090426
835510LV00043B/3248